Rece wants CEREAL

Written by:
Jasmine Poole

To my guys whom I love to the moon and back-

Son, you are a hero! Your life was always, and continues to be, my inspiration.

Big Rece, you are the epitome of an amazing Dad, you're MY ROCK!

I couldn't imagine traveling this road without you.

ISBN: 978-0692909898

Publisher: MDR Press

Printed in the U.S.A

iwalk4rece.com

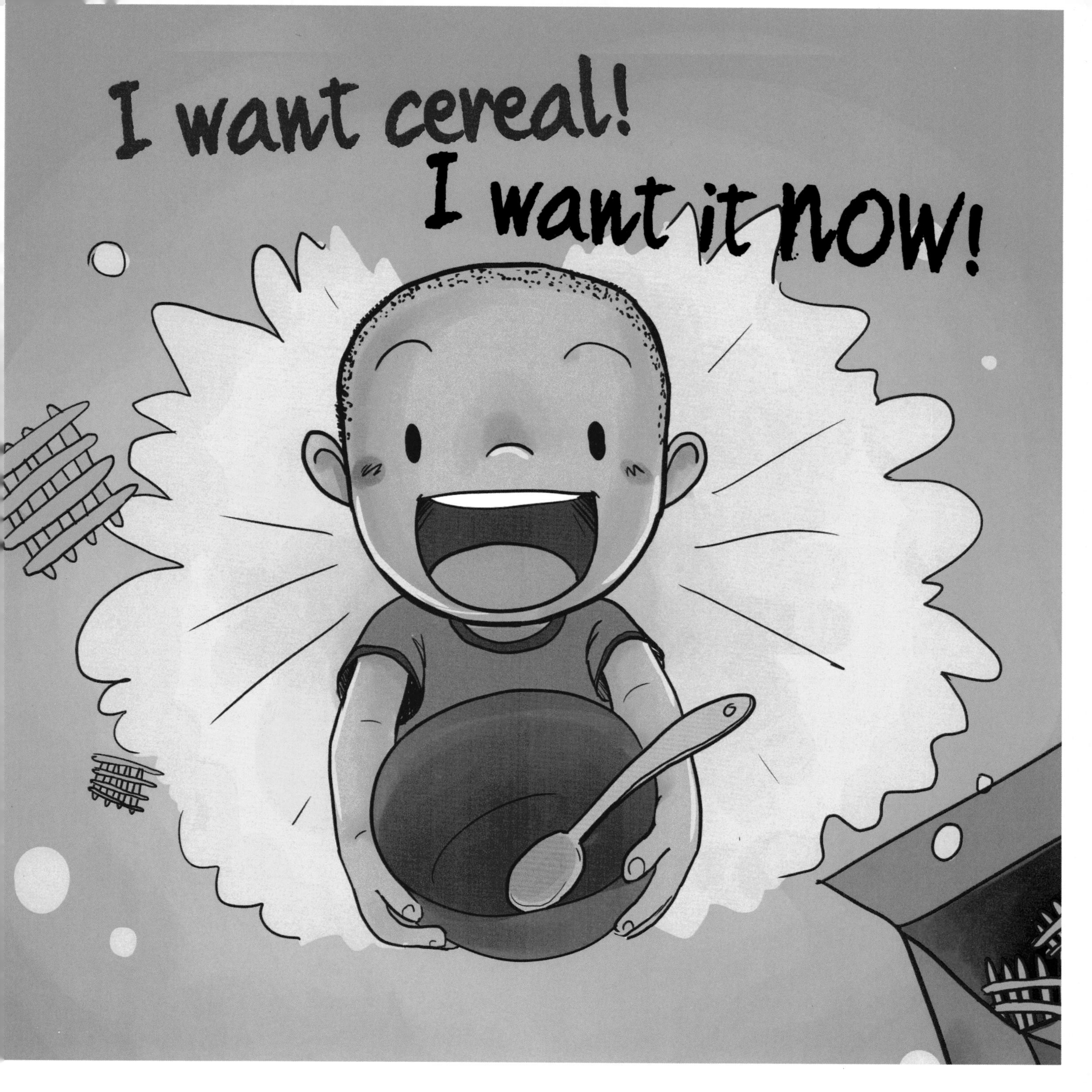
I want cereal!
I want it NOW!

the taste is
GREAT
on my tongue
I prefer to eat it
DRY—
ONE by ONE!

But my speech is different,

and that's not okay.

We smile and hug each other.
I'm proud I got my cereal too!

Autism is a developmental disorder that impacts a person's ability to communicate and socialize. Today autism remains a lifelong disorder with no solid answer as to why or how children are affected. Autism currently affects 1 in 68 children. It is the fastest growing developmental disorder in the U.S. There is no current cure.*

[*Information obtained from AutismSpeaks.org]

Pictured here: Jasmine Poole and her son, Rece.

Rece has autism and is non-verbal. His love for cereal has aided his ability to effectively communicate without the use of his voice. Currently Rece uses picture icons, modified sign language, and an augmented communication device to communicate. His parents believe that one day there will be solid answers to the puzzling mystery of autism. With this belief they walk every year with family and friends as team **"iWALK4Rece,"** in partnership with Autism Speaks. To date they have raised over $13,000 to help individuals with the same diagnosis.

Made in the USA
Columbia, SC
17 July 2017

Rece wants cereal! But he is completely non-verbal and unable to use his voice to tell his mom! What will he do? How will he get his precious cereal? Join Rece, a unique boy with autism, as he learns how to get what he truly wants in a whole new way.

ISBN 9780692909898

90000 >

9 780692 909898

I can tell mommy what I want
without getting frustrated

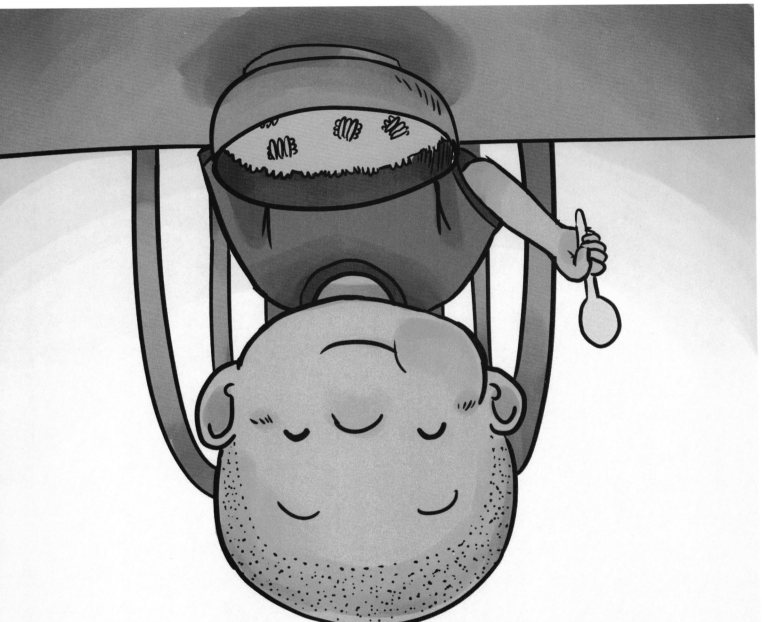

I sit in my seat
and treasure every single bite.

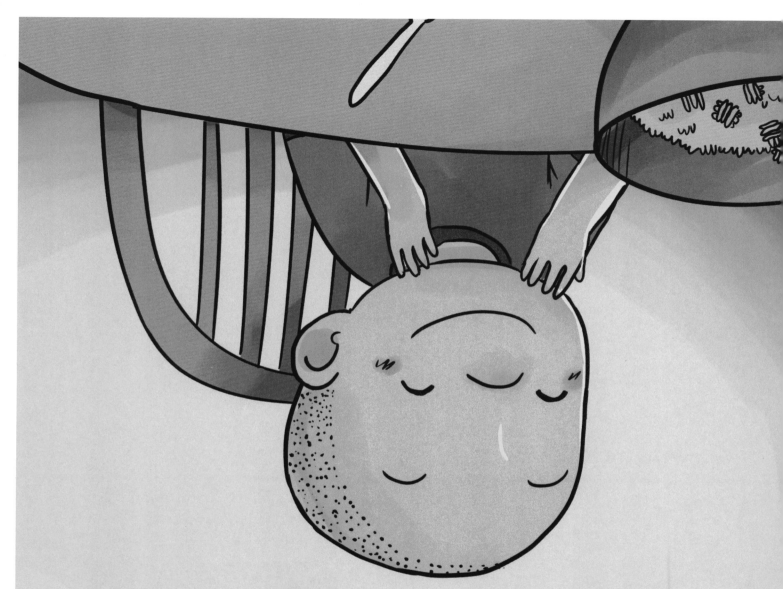

SHE UNDERSTANDS WHAT I WANT.
I giggle in delight

and pours it—
just enough,
not a lot.

There are so many ways
to communicate what I want to say

Mommy knows what I want,
but must I tell her another way?